Rescuers Defying The Nazis

Non-Jewish Teens Who Rescued Jews

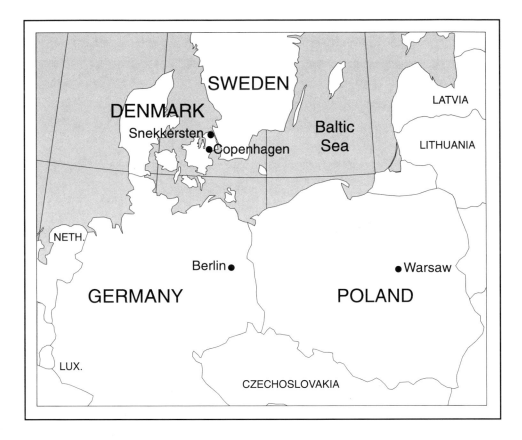

Most of Denmark's Jews were taken from the town of Snekkersten to safety in Sweden, a short boat ride away.

TEEN WITNESSES TO THE HOLOCAUST

Rescuers Defying The Nazis

Non-Jewish Teens Who Rescued Jews

Toby Axelrod

THE ROSEN PUBLISHING GROUP, INC.
NEW YORK

Dedicated to my grandfather, Conan Caron, who turned 102 this year and has been a lifelong inspiration. With profound thanks to my editor, Patra McSharry Sevastiades, and former colleague Fred Wasserman of the Luboml Exhibition Project, for their wisdom, friendship, and encouragment.

Published in 1999 by The Rosen Publishing Group, Inc.
29 East 21st Street, New York, New York 10010

First Edition

Library of Congress Cataloging-in-Publication Data

Axelrod, Toby.
    Rescuers defying the Nazis : Toby Axelrod.
        p.   cm. — (Teen witnesses to the Holocaust)
    Includes bibliographical references and index.
    Summary: Related the stories of courageous non-Jewish teenagers who rescued Jews from the Nazis.
    ISBN 0-8239-2848-9
    1. Righteous Gentiles in the Holocaust—Biography—Juvenile literature. 2. Holocaust, Jewish (1939–1945)—Juvenile literature.
3. World War, 1939–1945—Personal narratives—Juvenile literature.
4. Teenagers—Biography—Juvenile literature. [1. Righteous Gentiles in the Holocaust. 2. Holocaust, Jewish (1939–1945).
3. World War, 1939–1945—Personal narratives.]   I. Title.
II. Series.
D804.65A94 1998
362.87'81'0922—dc21
    [b]   98-43857
                                          CIP
                                          AC

Manufactured in the United States of America

Contents

Introduction   6

1. Chapter One   9

2. Antisemitism and War   12

3. Rescue as Resistance   20

4. Teresa Prekerowa   22

5. Preben Munch-Nielsen   26

6. Niels Bamberger   33

7. Ruth Winkler-Kühne   41

8. Honor and Controversy   48

9. Preserving the Memories   50

   Timeline   54

   Glossary   56

   For Further Reading   58

   Index   62

Introduction

It is important for everyone to learn about the Holocaust, the systematic murder of 6 million Jews during World War II (1939–1945). It is a dark scar across the face of human history. As a student, you are part of the future generation that will lead and guide the family of humankind. Your proper understanding of the Holocaust is essential. You will learn its lessons. You will be able to ensure that a Holocaust will never happen again and that the world will be a safe place for each person—regardless of his or her nationality, religion, or ethnicity.

Nazi Germany added a dangerous new element to the familiar concept of "dislike of the unlike." The Nazis introduced the idea that an *ethnic group* whom someone dislikes or hates can be isolated from the rest of the population and earmarked for total destruction, *without any possibility of survival.*

The Nazis chose the Jewish people for this fatal annihilation. Their definition of a Jew was a uniquely racial one: a person with Jewish blood. To the Nazis, a person with even one Jewish grandparent was a Jew—a person to be killed.

The Germans systematically rounded up Jews in the countries that they occupied during World War II. They built death camps equipped with the most sophisticated technology available in order to kill the Jews. With the assistance of collaborators (non-Germans who willingly helped), they murdered more than 6 million Jews. Among the victims were 1.5 million children and teenagers. These Jewish children, like Jewish adults, had no options. They were murdered because they had Jewish blood, and nothing they could do could change that.

Such a thing had never happened before in recorded history, despite the fact that genocide (deliberate destruction of people of one ethnic, political, or cultural group) had occurred. In the past, victims or oppressed people were usually offered an option to avoid death: they could change their religion, or be expelled to another country. But the Nazi concept of racism did not give the victim any possibility for survival, since a person cannot change his or her blood, skin color, or eye color.

A few non-Jewish people, known as the Righteous Among the Nations, saved Jews from death. They felt that they were their brothers' and sisters' keepers. But they were in the minority. The majority were collaborators or bystanders. During the Holocaust, I was a young child saved by several Righteous Poles. The majority of my family and the Jews of my town, many of whose families had lived there for 900 years, were murdered by the Nazis with the assistance of local collaborators. Photographs of those who were murdered gaze upon visitors to the Tower of Life exhibit that I created for the United States Holocaust Memorial Museum in Washington, D.C.

We must learn the lessons of the Holocaust. We must learn to respect one another, regardless of differences in religion, ethnicity, or race, since we all belong to the family of humankind. The United States and Canada are both countries of immigrants, populated by many ethnic groups. In lands of such diversity, dislike of the unlike—the Nazi idea of using racial classification as a reason to destroy other humans—is dangerous to all of us. If we allow intolerance toward one group of people today, any of us could be part of a group selected for destruction tomorrow. Understanding and respecting one another regardless of religion, race, or ethnicity is essential for coexistence and survival.

In this book individuals who were teenagers during the Holocaust share their experiences of life before and during the war and of the days of liberation. Their messages about their families, friends, love, suffering, survival, liberation, and rebuilding of new lives are deeply inspiring. They are important because these survivors are among the last eyewitnesses, the last links to what happened during the Holocaust.

I hope that their stories will encourage you to build a better, safer future "with liberty and justice for all."

Yaffa Eliach, Ph.D.
Professor of History and Literature
Department of Judaic Studies, Brooklyn College

chapter one

Jerzy Roslan was thirteen in 1943, when his parents hid three Jewish brothers—Jacob, David, and Shalom Gutgold—in their home in German-occupied Warsaw, Poland. The Roslans knew what could happen if they were discovered. The entire Roslan family would be hanged, recalls Jerzy's father, Alexander. For a few days, their bodies would hang on the balcony as a message to others who might dare to help Jews.

Despite the risk, Jerzy acted heroically. When he was hospitalized with scarlet fever, Jerzy split his dosage of medicine and held some of it for one of the Jewish boys, remembers his father. Jews were forbidden from being treated by non-Jewish doctors.

One of the Jewish brothers eventually died of the illness. But the others survived, with help from the medicine saved by Jerzy. A few years ago, Jacob and David Gutgold made sure the Roslans would always be remembered by having them designated "Righteous Among the Nations" at Yad Vashem, Israel's Holocaust memorial.

As for Alexander, he will always remember the courage of his son, Jerzy, who was killed in crossfire when he was fourteen. When Alexander thinks of his son, he cries.

This is only one story of a non-Jewish family who helped Jews during the Holocaust. Like Jerzy, teens in these families often played

Opposite: The hidden attic where Anne Frank usually wrote in her diary. Anne and her family were hidden by non-Jews in the Netherlands.

an important and responsible role in protecting Jews from the Nazis. Adults were most often responsible for making these dangerous decisions. But in their acts of kindness, they often involved their children, many of whom were teenagers.

Most of those who rescued Jews did so out of a sense of social or religious responsibility or because it just seemed like the right thing to do. When asked, most say they did not think they were doing anything extraordinary. They simply could not stand by and watch their friends and neighbors suffer.

But it was not easy to defy the Nazis, and not many people took the risk. Imagine hiding people in your attic when you know that your neighbors have been shot for doing the same thing.

Imagine having your parents tell you that you must never speak about the hidden guests to anyone.

Imagine going to bed hungry after sharing scarce food with starving refugees.

Imagine worrying that someone might betray you.

Imagine the fear of hearing a knock on the door in the dead of night, of having the people you have hidden discovered, of all of you being taken away.

Still, people took these chances and more. Such people were rare to begin with. Today, they are still more rare, because, like the Holocaust survivors they helped, they are aging. But there are people alive today who remember what those difficult days were like. Many were teenagers then, as were many of those they saved.

Teens During the Holocaust

Europe was in upheaval during World War II. For teenagers, years that would normally be spent struggling for self-identity were also

10

Background: German army and air force personnel, along with Polish civilians, observe the hanging of seven Poles in the railyard of the Cracow-Plaszow train station.

spent grappling with concepts of good and evil. Many teens witnessed persecution and atrocities in their own hometowns. They saw their former doctor forced to give up his office. Sometimes, they saw German police forcing Jewish neighbors to clean the streets on their hands and knees. And ultimately, they saw Jewish friends fleeing for their lives—or even killed on the spot.

The Third Reich, as Hitler called his dictatorship, meant the suspension of a normal life. Instead of worrying about what class to take in school or which movie to see, teen witnesses were faced with deciding which authorities to heed: their parents and their own consciences, or the commands of a totalitarian dictator. They had to grow up quickly.

Before the war began in 1939, Hitler had already established antisemitic policies in Germany. Signs with such messages as "Beware of Jews and pickpockets" had become common in Germany. Jewish students were forbidden to attend school with non-Jews and had to stay indoors at night. Soon all Jews had to wear a yellow star sewn to their clothing. It was the beginning of the destruction of European Jewry by Adolf Hitler and his followers.

During the Third Reich it took great courage for a non-Jewish teen to remain loyal to a Jewish friend—especially when one could be severely punished for doing so.

Once Germany was at war, citizens of all occupied lands were forbidden to help Jews. Anyone caught hiding Jews might be executed, along with their entire family and the people they were trying to save.

Despite such horrible threats, families shared scarce food with Jews hiding under a barn floor, hid friends in an attic, or helped to shuttle people across borders under cover of night. Many of those rescuers who survived the war have been honored for their sacrifice by Yad Vashem, Israel's memorial to the Holocaust. They are known as Righteous Among the Nations, or Righteous Gentiles.

This book describes the experiences of a few young people who participated in the effort to save Jews from the Nazis. Their courage is an inspiration.

chapter two

In January 1933, Hitler became chancellor of Germany. Only a few months earlier, Hitler's political party, the National Socialists, or Nazis, had won one-third of all votes in a national election. They had not won a majority, but they had enough votes to beat all the other parties.

For his supporters, Hitler represented a chance to win back some of the respect Germany had lost after its defeat in World War I. At the end of that war, in 1918, Germany was forced to pay reparations for the rebuilding of the countries it had attacked. At the same time, many people in Germany were jobless. Many of them thought that Germany didn't deserve to be punished for the war. At any rate, critics said, the punishment seemed too harsh.

People who voted for Hitler hoped he would live up to his promises: to bring jobs and prosperity back to Germany. But Hitler said more than that: Knowing that many Germans were depressed about losing World War I, he decided to uplift his people by claiming Germans were the smartest, strongest, most beautiful human beings. He referred to Germans and Austrians as members of an "Aryan"

Adolf Hitler during the elections of 1932–33.

Crowds in Nuremberg, Germany give the Nazi salute, September 1938.

race, superior to every other race on earth.

Of course, if Hitler believed that Germans were perfect, he also believed that Germany's problems had to be someone else's fault. For Hitler, it was not hard to find a scapegoat, or a people on whom to blame these problems. Through his young adulthood, Hitler had been developing a theory that all problems could be blamed on Jewish people. Now that he was in power, he focused much of his attention on developing policies that would make German Jews want to leave the country. Ultimately, Hitler's plans called for the killing of all Jews. The Nazis even planned a museum, which would have been dedicated to an "extinct" people.

The museum was to have been in Prague, in what is now the Czech

Republic. During World War II, the Nazis sent Jewish religious objects to a warehouse in Prague. These objects had been looted by German police and soldiers from synagogues and Jewish homes across Europe.

Hitler's Brand of Antisemitism

To Germans who had read Hitler's book, *Mein Kampf*—meaning *My Struggle*—his antisemitic leanings were no surprise. Hitler had written that the government must protect the "German race." He said that people of the Germanic race, "Aryans," were destined to take over the world. He said Judaism was not a religion but a means to control the world.

In Germany in the 1930s, most Jews were not very religious. Jews lived and worked alongside other Germans and were proud of their German heritage. In fact, Germany boasts one of the oldest Jewish communities in Europe. In contrast to the Jews of Germany in the 1930s, many Jews who lived in Eastern Europe —including Poland and Hungary—and the former Soviet Union were more religious. They were more likely to live in small towns, close to other Jewish people. They often spoke Yiddish, a Jewish dialect of German, and used Polish or Russian or Ukrainian, for example,

The facial features of a young German are measured during a "racial examination" at the Kaiser Wilhelm Institute for Anthropology. The Nazis believed that such examinations could indicate who was truly "Aryan."

in their interactions with citizens who were not Jewish.

Hitler's hatred of Jews eventually would reach beyond the borders of his own country. But in his early days in power, Hitler sounded like many other Germans who blamed Germany's economic problems on the Jews.

The Nazis Take Power

Soon after he was elected, Hitler gave himself a lot of powers. He took control of the police and the newspapers, and used them to spread his ideas and enforce his restrictions.

The Nazis uplifted German teens who fit the "Aryan" stereotype. At the same time, they enacted laws that curtailed the rights of Jews. Little by little, Jews were forced to give up jobs, property, and businesses. Jewish students were forced into special Jewish schools.

Sometimes people who spoke up in defense of Jewish friends or

A German civilian wearing a Nazi armband holds signs urging shoppers to boycott Jewish shops as members of Hitler's *Sturmabteilung*, or "storm troops," paste them on the windows of a Jewish-owned business.

neighbors would be punished by the police. Very quickly, the average German citizen learned how dangerous it could be to help Jews.

The Nuremberg Laws of 1935 put Hitler's attack on Jews into the German legal code. The laws prohibited marriages between Jews and non-Jews. Anyone with one Jewish parent was considered a "mixed breed," or *Mischling*. Anyone with at least one Jewish grandparent was considered Jewish.

Kristallnacht

On the night of November 9–10, 1938, the Nazi policy of antisemitism went wild. In one German city after another, and even in small towns, synagogues were burned and Jewish-owned businesses were looted and destroyed. That night came to be called Kristallnacht, or the night of broken glass.

Instead of protecting private property, many police officers stood by and even participated in this attack, which also took place in Austria. Hundreds of synagogues were destroyed, some 100 Jews were murdered, and 30,000 Jewish men were imprisoned in German concentration camps on that day.

After that, many German Jews who could afford to buy tickets on ships or trains left their homeland for other countries. By mid-1939, about 300,000 Jews had managed to leave. Many of those who remained, or who thought they had escaped to safe ground elsewhere in Europe, would later fall victim to the Nazis.

More than 90 percent of German Jews who remained were sent to concentration camps, where they were killed or forced into slave labor. Of the remaining 10 percent, many were saved by individuals who risked their lives to hide Jews.

Germany Begins the War

World War II began on September 1, 1939, when Germany invaded Poland. Hitler's goal was to attach Poland to Germany, creating more room for Germans. To accomplish this goal, non-Aryans had to be removed, said Hitler.

Meanwhile, the German army invaded and occupied several

Opposite: A view of the interior of the Essenweinstrasse synagogue after its destruction during Kristallnacht. Nuremberg, Germany.

other European countries. In Poland and elsewhere in Eastern Europe, the Nazis gradually ordered all the Jews to be relocated into heavily guarded ghettos. There, thousands of people were confined in overcrowded, unheated buildings, without sufficient food, medicine, or clothing. By concentrating the Jews together, the Nazis made it easier to use them for slave labor or to deport them in large numbers to concentration camps.

As the war progressed, the Nazis would try to round up all the so-called occupied. These "undesirables" included Jews, Roma and Sinti people ("Gypsies"), homosexuals, and people with mental and physical disabilities. The Nazis, often helped by local people, would either kill large groups of Jews outright or send them to concentration camps, where they would be worked to death or killed.

By 1945, when Germany surrendered, the Nazis had occupied most of Europe, including parts of Scandinavia and the former Soviet Union. Some nine million Jews had lived in those areas before the war. By spring 1945, some six million had been murdered in mass executions or in death camps.

A German police officer kicks a Jew who is climbing onto the back of a truck during a roundup for forced labor. Other German officers look on scornfully.

chapter three

Rescue as Resistance

In every occupied country there were collaborators, people who willingly assisted the Germans, and resisters, those who actively opposed them. Rescuing Jews was one of the most dangerous forms of resistance, because it was usually punishable by death. Often, rescuers said afterward that they did not think about the danger.

Many European Jews who survived did so with the help of non-Jews. In fact, more than 10,000 individuals have been honored as Righteous Among the Nations by Yad Vashem, Israel's Holocaust memorial.

Many rescuers were teens

Three Danes who helped in the rescue of Danish Jews.

Eyewitness accounts by survivors have led to recognition for many as Righteous Gentiles. There are strict guidelines to be met in order to be honored by Yad Vashem. For example:
- a rescuer must have helped a Jew in danger of being killed
- he or she must have been aware of the risk to his or her own life
- he or she cannot have asked for any payment at the time of the rescue, but it was okay to accept financial help if it was offered

with their lives ahead of them. Some acted alone while others took part in an underground network. Sometimes rescuers provided medicine and false identity papers, such as passports, or food and shelter. At other times, they provided "safe houses," hiding Jews until they could safely be moved to other safe houses and finally to freedom.

Some people hid Jews in attics, barns, underground cellars, even under pigstics. In some cases Jewish children were hidden in monasteries or convents. They took on false identities, posing as Christians.

The total number of Righteous Gentiles may never be known, but many estimates put the figure at about 50,000—less than one percent of the 200 million non-Jews in Europe during the Third Reich.

Most rescuers were in Poland, which also contained the largest share of Europe's pre-Holocaust Jewish population.Rescuers there are credited with having saved a significant number of Jews.

chapter four

Teresa Prekerowa

Polish historian Teresa Prekerowa was born in 1921. She lived with her parents, three brothers, and one sister in Warsaw. During Germany's war with Poland, one of her brothers had been captured and executed by the Germans. Another brother was interned in a military camp. So Teresa's parents, Halina and Waclaw, were very worried about their other children. That is why Teresa did not tell them when she rescued a little girl in Nazi-occupied Warsaw. She knew it was dangerous, but she did it anyway.

I was a student studying history. I think it was October 1942. It was about eight o'clock in the evening. It was cold and dark, and it was raining. There was almost nobody in the street. The public could only be in the street until eight o'clock in the evening, so I was going very quickly home.

In addition to imposing a curfew on all of the citizens of Warsaw, the Nazis had forcibly moved the Jews of Warsaw into a part of the city designated as a ghetto, in November 1940. Teresa lived about a mile away from the ghetto.

Above: German tanks enter a Polish village during the invasion of Poland, September 1939.

But then I heard something—it was a little girl who was crying. She was standing in the entrance of a house at Mokotovska Street. It was a narrow street. It was not near the ghetto, it was near my home. She was begging for somebody to help her. She was standing in the doorway and crying. I think maybe she was three or four years old. She was wearing very, very poor clothes. And I looked at her, and I saw at once she was Jewish.

I think she had come with her mother, because when I took the girl's hand I felt that someone was watching us. I think it was her mother. I was feeling that I had to help her, but I knew that it was terribly dangerous and I was afraid. It was only a little question in my mind. Not long. I had to decide at once.

It was not a long way to my home, and so I took her. It was difficult. If somebody saw me at this moment—some German, of course—it was very dangerous. People who got caught helping Jews didn't come back home. The Germans would paste an announcement on the wall with the names of fifteen or twenty people who were put to death for helping Jews.

Two destitute children in the Warsaw ghetto

But I took her and went with her to my home. I lived together with my father and mother but they were away with my sister and my other brother, so I was alone. My younger brother Jerzy had been put to death in a German prison by the Nazis, and my elder brother Andrzej was interned in a Nazi military camp and we didn't know what happened to him. So my father and mother were terribly anxious about my other brother and my sister and me. They didn't want me to do something that could be dangerous. That is why I knew I could not tell them what I did.

When the young woman and the little girl arrived at Teresa's home, Teresa put her finger to her lips. The little girl understood her gesture and took care to be quiet.

She was very frightened. She didn't know Polish, only Yiddish. So I had to teach her how to say "bread." I taught her to say Catholic prayers, and how to say her name. I said to her, "You are Anja." I didn't know her real name because she didn't say it. And so I gave her something to eat, I bathed her. But her clothes were impossible to show in the street. So I went the next day to my friend who had a little girl and asked her to give me some old clothes, because it was impossible for me to buy her new clothes. I had no money.

Teresa kept Anja inside, but she knew she could not keep her hidden for long. Her family was due back in several days. She was already putting her family at risk by keeping the girl in their apartment and could not expose them to further danger.

Anja learned very quickly. It was not possible for such a little girl to speak fluently, so I didn't have to teach much. But after one week, she had learned to pray and say, "I am Anja."

And then I took her to the convent. Since she didn't speak Polish, it was impossible to explain to her where and why she was going. I only told her, "You will be safe there. The Germans will not come to that house."

The nuns were called Nazaretanki (Sisters of Nazareth), in Warsaw, on Czerniakowska Street. I didn't know if the sisters would agree to take her. So I put a card in her hand that said, "I am Anja, my parents don't exist anymore, please give me help."

She seemed upset and afraid but did not cry. I disappeared quickly, but I went to a nearby street to see if she will stay in the convent or if they will put her out the door. Once she was in, nobody appeared at the door. After one hour, I saw she would stay there, and I left. I was sure they would take care of her. It was a sorrowful moment. I had grown fond of her.

Two times, I looked over the fence of the convent from the street. I saw the girl playing and a nun caressing her. That reassured me; I felt that I made the right choice. After the war, I went to the convent to ask what happened. They didn't remember this special case, but they said that the Germans did not take anyone. All the girls survived.

The Nazaretanki (Sisters of Nazareth) convent in Warsaw, Poland.

chapter five

Preben Munch-Nielsen

Preben Munch-Nielsen was born in 1926 in Denmark. He and his four siblings were raised by their grandmother in the coastal town of Snekkersten. Preben (PREH-bin) was fourteen years old in 1940, when the Germans occupied his country. Snekkersten, only a few miles by boat from Sweden, became an escape route for Jews in fall 1943, when Germany ordered that Danish Jews be rounded up and deported.

Preben was one of the young Danes to risk his life ferrying refugees to safety in boats across the Øresund sound to neutral Sweden. He was also one of the teens who acted on his own, and not to help his parents. He did not think about the danger. He has always believed there was only one thing to do: to help other human beings.

I was brought up by my grandmother. It was a completely normal life. I went to school, played soccer, went sailing. I was a scout. In Denmark, we had had freedom for hundreds of years. We had a good life.

The German Invasion

The Germans invaded Denmark in 1940.

On the morning of April 9, 1940, there were hundreds of airplanes overhead. I'd never seen that before. They came over us, and everyone looked up. That was shocking. Then when I went to school, in Copenhagen, twenty-five miles away by train, and there were German soldiers everywhere, that was a shock. We never thought they would come to Denmark.

At first, the occupiers did not change life very much, but their presence was deeply resented. The Danish government, parliament, army, navy, and civil service were allowed to keep functioning. Gradually, though, freedoms were eroded. The media were censored, and only a German version of the news was available.

We were not allowed to sail in the sound between Denmark and Sweden anymore. The Germans were afraid we would escape. The only people allowed to sail in those days were fishermen. The Nazi occupation was a shock. We had never been occupied before, and then suddenly we were occupied by people who do things we cannot accept. So there was no choice. We had to do something.

German troops march into Denmark, 1940.

The Resistance

Preben was fifteen when he started working for the Resistance, people who secretly organized together to work against the Nazis. The Resistance published illegal pamphlets and later illegal weekly or monthly magazines. They reported the information that could not be printed in the legal newspapers. Preben was inspired by a teacher, Frode Jacobsen, and became a messenger delivering uncensored newsletters.

Some Danes were trained in England to carry out various kinds of sabotage and returned to Denmark in 1941. The primary targets for sabotage were Danish factories and workshops manufacturing items for the Germans. They were targeted to undercut the German war effort and to scare off Danes willing to cooperate with the Nazis. German ships under construction in Denmark were damaged. Ships bound for Germany often had "tortoises" attached: explosives containing magnets that could stick to the side of a ship.

The Danes put up so much resistance that the German Reich commissioner in Denmark, Dr. Werner Best, consulted Hitler about it. Then on August 28, 1943, Best demanded that the Danish government impose the death penalty for the crime of sabotage. The government refused. The following night, the Germans disarmed the Danish army and seized control of the navy. The Danes sank their own naval ships so that they would not fall into German hands. The Danish government retired, and the Gestapo took over.

Danish Resistance fighters on a rooftop.

Dr. Best recommended that the persecution of Jews begin in Denmark. The roundup was planned to begin on October 1, the second day of Rosh Hashanah, the Jewish New Year.

Outwitting the Nazis

The German maritime attaché in Denmark, G. F. Duckwitz, learned of the plan to deport Denmark's 8,000 Jews. The Nazis planned the deportation for October 1, 1943. In September, Duckwitz leaked this information to Danish politicians, who passed it on to the Jewish community. Preben learned of it from a police officer.

The Jews in Denmark were our fellow citizens. They did not live in special ghettos. They were our next-door neighbors. It was not a topic for discussion. There was no difference between us.

The Danish Resistance acted quickly. By September 29, the eve of the Jewish New Year, almost all the Jews of Denmark were hiding in non-Jewish homes, in hospitals, or in other institutions. Later, they were brought to fishing ports on the sound. Snekkersten, Preben's hometown, was one of them.

A Resistance leader asked Preben to guide some Jews from the train station to the shore. Preben did not have a photograph to go by, but it was not difficult for him to identify the fleeing travelers: they were not from Snekkersten, and they looked uncertain as to which direction to take. But the Nazis—who wrongly believed that Jews all had a similar "look"—could not distinguish them from other Danes.

Over the next few months, Preben helped ferry Jews across the three-mile Øresund to Sweden. Since only fishermen could sail in the sound, the Danish Resistance secretly arranged to transport the Danish Jews in fishing boats.

A member of the Resistance bought a boat. He claimed it was stolen so the former owner would not get in trouble for being involved with the Resistance. We got the boat down to the sea, and it was hidden in Sweden in the daytime.

Many fishermen volunteered their boats as well. Refugees hid in the boats, under fishing nets and inside the hold, trying to remain silent when German police would board for an inspection. Remarkably, of the seven thousand Jews ferried across the sound to Sweden, no one was ever discovered.

A Well-Organized Operation

We didn't know the full awful truth about the concentration camps, but we knew so much that we could imagine the fate of our fellow citizens. We had heard about the "Final Solution." There was no doubt. You had nothing else to do but do what you could in order to avoid that the Germans succeed in their plans.

Once Preben started helping, he never thought of stopping.

There were so many jobs involved. We had to pick the refugees up at a train station, we brought them to houses, helped them down to the shore. You could not afford to be afraid. And if you were, you could not let it have any impact on what you had to do.

Friends would signal when it was safe to leave. There were even some German soldiers who pretended not to see, according to historical accounts. In good weather, the trip across the sound could take as little as twenty minutes. But then it would also be easier for a German boat to catch up. So Preben preferred choppy waters. The Resistance members never carried guns, partly because they knew they could not win a gun battle with the German patrol, and if they were caught with guns, they might be shot immediately. If they didn't have guns, they might instead be sent to one of the concentration camps in Denmark.

Luckily, Preben never had any close calls. Members of the Resistance helped each other by watching out for German patrol boats and warning each other by telephone.

Everything was done in order to minimize the risk. That was one of the reasons why everything went rather perfectly.

Late in 1943, a member of the Resistance warned Preben to remain in Sweden. He did. Later, the Snekkersten innkeeper who had begun the secret boat trips, Henry Thomsen, was arrested by the Gestapo and sent to a concentration camp, where he died.

Undiminished Hope

In the spring of 1944, Preben joined the Danish Brigade in Sweden, which trained Danes to prepare

Danish fishing boats.

to fight the Germans. A year later, the war in Europe was over.

I returned home on the fifth of May, 1945, the same day the war ended in Denmark. It was really wonderful. I was happy to have survived, happy to see my family, happy to see that my country was not destroyed. On the shore there were lots of people. Denmark went amok that night.

Only 477 Danish Jews had been captured by the Nazis. They were all sent to Theresienstadt, a concentration camp near Prague, in Czechoslovakia (now the Czech Republic). About 417 survived.

Today, Preben doesn't want to be thanked for what he did. And many Danes feel the same, he says.

We don't believe in innocent bystanders. Because if you see something and do nothing, then you are not innocent anymore. Then you have taken sides. And that would be in favor of the evil.

chapter six

Niels Bamberger was born in October 1928 in Würzburg, Germany. He and his parents fled Germany to Copenhagen, Denmark, which had been his mother's home until 1932. In Copenhagen, his father opened an art store.

We had a house in the center of Copenhagen. It had belonged to my grandfather and great-grandfather. It's still standing. And it's probably two or three hundred years old. We lived in a big apartment on the second floor. There were other people living in the house and stores on the ground floor. And we had a synagogue that had been there for more than one hundred years, started by my great-grandfather, in the same house.

I was brought up very Orthodox, and, of course, my parents were too. My grandfather was a rabbi, and my brother is a rabbi today. So that's the way we grew up.

We had services every day in our synagogue. The reason our synagogue was started originally by my great-grandfather was that he thought that the big synagogue—they have a beautiful, large synagogue in Copenhagen—wasn't Orthodox enough. They started with different reformed things: they cut this prayer out, and they cut this one out.

Opposite: Members of the Holger Danske, a Danish underground force, outside headquarters in Copenhagen, May 12, 1945.

That's when my great-grandfather started his own synagogue, so to speak. It still can be seen. It's in the museum in Copenhagen.

I went to a non-Jewish school. I wouldn't say I was the only Jew in school. We were probably two or three fellows. In the afternoon, we went to Hebrew school for another two or three hours. We came home at about 5:30 or 6:00 every night and did our homework. And that was the same routine. Then we were off and we went to football games and bicycling and things like that with my friends.

My Christian neighbors were my friends. We went together for this or for that, and we had birthday parties, and we went to ball games. There was no difference. Nobody ever mentioned anything about being Jewish or non-Jewish. We were citizens of Denmark, and that's all they cared about.

A loudspeaker truck passes through a Danish town announcing that Germany has occupied Denmark, April 29, 1940.

Denmark Is Occupied

When the Germans invaded in 1940, Niels was twelve years old.

We were in school that day. We saw loads and loads of planes, bombing planes, hundreds and hundreds of planes coming in, and Germans on motorcycles and horses, dragging cannons and big tanks all over the place. It didn't take more than a couple of hours until they took over the country.

Life went on as before, except that we were not allowed to walk on this side of the street in front of the bank. The Germans would post soldiers with guns and steel helmets in front of the banks and the hotels and important institutions that they wanted to guard. But besides that, nothing happened really. Everything got rationed: butter, bread, and gasoline. You couldn't go out and buy whatever you wanted, but there was plenty of it around. The Germans took away whatever they needed, but there was still plenty.

Then in August 1943, the Germans arrested all the police and the army. They interned them in camps and took their weapons away. That's when we knew something was going to happen.

Going into Hiding

On October 1—it was the second day of Rosh Hashanah—the Germans picked up all the files from the Jewish community centers. They had all the names and addresses of everyone in Copenhagen, about 6,000 Jews. They knew where they lived, what they did, their business. They had everything.

In the synagogue on the first day of Rosh Hashanah, we were informed that nobody should go home because the Germans are going to round you up on the night between the first and second of October. Those who believed it, which most of the people did, were all scared. They didn't go home. We all made arrangements with some non-Jews where we could stay or where to sleep.

We went to our grocer, who was a bachelor, and

A group of Nazi soldiers stand at the doorway of a Jewish house.

37

he said, "Come to my house, and I'll take care of you." After synagogue, we went to him, and he brought us bread and butter and cheese and milk and eggs, whatever we needed. He took care of us for a week until we found a connection to get out of the country. We were six people altogether.

Every day our grocer called up somebody that he knew from the Resistance movement. He wouldn't say that he has some people to send, because he didn't know if his telephone was tapped. So he called up and said, "I have six tons of potatoes. Could you come and pick them up?"

The grocer found a connection for Niels's family. They were going to escape Denmark from Snekkersten.

We got a taxi. We were covered up with a blanket in case the police would stop and say, "What's wrong? What do you have in there?" The driver would say, "I have a sick person. Just close the door. I have to go to the hospital." It's not more than a thirty- or forty-minute ride by taxi to Snekkersten, where everybody had been collected. We came to a certain house. There were two or three or four hundred people there every day in somebody's home, in a basement.

When it got dark, somebody led Niels's family down to the pier. When they arrived, Niels recalls, they were told that the boat they were supposed to have gone on had been taken by somebody else who had paid more money for it.

So we had to wait until the next night. Luckily for us, the Resistance movement had a big schooner-like ship, and they took two or three hundred people aboard. We went out there by rowboat. It wasn't far out to the ship. We all went down below deck.

When they had all the people there, we paid them money. We paid like 2,000 krone [about $300] a person. Which was a lot of money at that time, but we were told if you come to Sweden the money would be worthless. Second, whatever money you give now will help those people who are poor or sick and can't afford to get out of Denmark. Everybody got out, whether they had money or not.

We sailed for an hour or so at midnight. In the middle of the Øresund, we had this big torpedo boat or gunboat coming towards us.

We all thought it was the Germans, but it was a Swedish boat. They helped us all off our ship and onto the Swedish ship. They gave us coffee and candy or whatever, and then we went into Sweden. And we were saved.

Seeking Safety, Again

When Niels and his family landed in Sweden, they were all registered by the Swedish authorities. They had arrived in Sweden the day before Yom Kippur, the holiest day of the Jewish calendar and a day of fasting. They had only the clothes on their backs.

In Sweden we got food. We got clothing. We went to a big camp that was guarded by Swedish soldiers, and we could come and go freely. My father wanted to go to the synagogue, which was ten or twelve miles away in Hälsingborg.

Niels's family walked all the way to Hälsingborg because Orthodox Jews do not ride in vehicles on Yom Kippur.

We attended the services, a full day of services, without food. In the middle of the afternoon, a girl came in with a big bus, and they interrupted the services. They said that all the people from Denmark, all the refugees who are here in the synagogue, should immediately come out to the bus and go back to camp. My father said, "Now that we have been saved from the Germans, we are not going to go on a bus on Yom Kippur."

39

We waited until after the services were over at night, and then somebody drove us back to the camp from the synagogue. And when we came back to camp, we were told, "You have to leave tonight because you didn't come back with the girl who was sent with the bus." We had no money. So we went to the railroad station. And somebody bought us the tickets to Malmö, where my father had a cousin. We arrived there in the middle of the night, two or three o'clock in the morning. We were very lucky. We were saved. We were happy.

Niels's family eventually found their own apartment and started a restaurant. Niels, who was fifteen, worked in a flower shop as a delivery boy to make extra money.

We were very happy there. We were there for close to two years, until May 1945. On the 28th of May everybody went back on the ferry boats to Denmark. And when we came back to Denmark, we all got money. Not a lot of money, but some money.

And I remember we came home to our apartment and found everything the way we had left it—except, of course, there were mice and spiders and all kinds of things. But the food was on the table, still in the pots. Nobody had been into the apartment. Everything was the way we left it. And the synagogue that I mentioned before, our lawyer had taken away the Torah scrolls and hidden them in a vault in a bank. And they were all left the way we had left them two years earlier.

The return of Danish Jews to Denmark from Sweden, May 1945.

chapter seven

Ruth Winkler was born in 1931 and lived in Trebbin, Germany, with her parents, Hans and Frida, and her brother Horst, who was two years older.

Starting in the summer of 1943, when Ruth was twelve, Hans and Frida Winkler hid a Jewish teenager, Eugen Herman-Friede, in their two-room house in Luckenwalde, a town near Berlin with a wartime population of about 35,000. Eugen, who was sixteen, stayed with the Winklers until December 1944.

Eugen Herman-Friede was born in 1926. He grew up in Berlin. His birth parents were Jewish, but his mother had divorced his father (Moses Herman) and remarried (Julius Friede) when Eugen was very young. Her second husband was a non-religious Christian. They tried to go through a formal

Frida and Ruth Winkler, around 1943–1944.

adoption process so Eugen could be Julius' son. But they did not succeed. In the summer of 1943, Eugen was hiding in the Winkler home. His parents were in the attic of a nearby inn.

During the year in hiding, Ruth Winkler and her brother, Horst, had to protect Eugen from the eyes of strangers and even other family members. Their parents also started a resistance group.

Called the Association for Peace and Reconstruction, it was founded in the autumn of 1943 by Hans Winkler, Ruth's father, an employee of the courts in his town, and Werner Scharff. Scharff, who was Jewish, had been one of the very few people to escape from Theresienstadt concentration camp. Scharff reported that Jews were being killed in the camps. The Association committed itself to printing leaflets opposing the Nazi regime and calling for an end to the war.

Ruth and her brother helped to mail these leaflets. Ruth knew it was dangerous for anyone outside the immediate family to know what they were doing. But the family also knew that Jews were in danger for their lives.

I came home one day and Eugen was there. I said to my father, "Who is this?"

Father said, "This is your cousin."

But I knew all my cousins. I told my mother, "This is not my cousin."

My mother said, "I will explain tomorrow."

The next morning, she explained to me that he was Jewish and if anyone found him

Ruth's father, Hans Winkler, 1942.

he would be taken away like my father's friend Günther Samuel. Günther Samuel's whole family was taken away. My mother said, "If anyone asks, you must always say this is your cousin." We were not allowed to go against the stream, openly.

Keeping a Secret

Most of our relatives never even saw Eugen's face. To those who did, my mother said, "He is a distant relative." The house had to be dark at night, so people could not look into a window and see Eugen. It was a new building, and one could hear through the walls when one used the toilet. If water was running, someone in the next apartment heard.

When guests came over, Eugen hid in the wardrobe. If someone came in without warning, he hid behind the wardrobe. A coat hung over the side, so no one could see him.

Even when the family came to visit, we were happy when they were gone again. We wished that they would go. It was a small town, and someone once in a while would come by to say hello, but we were happy when they didn't talk too long. You might not even be safe with family. My mother had many sisters, who were married and had children. And they were rather in favor of Hitler. They had all been jobless, and when Hitler came to power they had jobs.

The only thing people said about Jews in Luckenwalde was that it was "good that they are out of our city." Many Jews had emigrated and others were taken away, and the citizens were happy that the Jews had gone away.

On Kristallnacht, November 9 and 10, 1938, Jewish property was vandalized in Luckenwalde as everywhere in Germany.

There was a shoe store, and I saw the window broken and there was a sign, "Don't buy from Jews." I was with my parents. They took us children, they wanted us to see. My father said, "Look at what they did there to these Jewish people who have lived in this town for decades." For me it was a shock.

Pretending to Support the Führer

Ruth and her brother had to appear to be normal German teens on the outside. So Horst was a member of the Hitler Youth, and Ruth was in the Bund Deutsche Mädel (BDM), or League of German Girls.

All girls from the age of ten had to belong. We had to attend meetings every week, and we learned about Hitler and the Fatherland. We learned about how the British and the Americans were bombing our ships. We had to be good Germans. The Führer *[the leader], Hitler, came first. Even before family. We had to believe in him more than in our parents.*

If you saw a teacher on the street, you must say "Heil Hitler" to him. At the entrance of the school, there was a teacher or principal standing there, and all the children must pass by and put their hand up and say "Heil Hitler."

Ruth had to give up her friendships. Her family's secret was too dangerous for anyone to know.

Before the war, we used to go in the street and play ball. When someone's parents had enough money to buy them a bicycle, we would say, "Wow, that is cool!" and in the winter we went ice skating. There was a small lake in Luckenwalde.

Before the war, we had a nice childhood. Our parents often went for walks with us in the woods, and we had a small garden. But then the war came, and the "Hitler greetings" began. But our parents trusted us. They said, We are family. They never thought we would denounce them for hiding Eugen.

Eugen was always with us, but there were a few other Jewish people who stayed overnight at other times.

Since my brother and I were over twelve, my mother had to work in a factory. My father was a court officer. We were home alone. I was never to let a stranger

Members of the
Hitler Youth, a
Nazi youth
organization,
saluting.

45

in the house. If someone came to the door, I would say, "My parents are not at home. I am sorry, I am alone in the house, I cannot let anyone in."

In 1943 and 1944, Hans Winkler and friends in the Resistance printed thousands of leaflets calling on Germans to passively resist the Nazi regime and to oppose the war. Eugen wrote addresses on the leaflets, and they were dropped off in post boxes in various cities. Ruth remembers mailing some leaflets from a train station in Dresden.

I was not worried. I thought no one would arrest me for sending mail. But then I was nervous later on, when I read in the newspapers and heard on the radio that people in the Resistance were being arrested. I heard they were sentencing these people to death after a show trial.

Arrests

A member of the Association, Hilde Bromberg, was arrested and tortured in April 1944. Soon, arrests of other members followed. Eugen left his hiding place with the Winklers and moved in with his parents. As more arrests followed, Eugen moved again. Meanwhile, Ruth's father was imprisoned in October 1944.

When my father was imprisoned, the Gestapo came and did a house search. They asked if anyone lived with us, and I said no.

After a few weeks in his new hiding place, Eugen felt safe enough to check on his parents. They were fine. The three had been together for about a week when they were raided in December 1944. All were arrested and taken to prison. The fact that they were Christian converts never came up, Eugen says. They were first beaten and robbed by the young Gestapo men (one of whom Eugen knew) who raided their hiding place. They were then brought to prison.

Eugen was separated from his parents and ended up in a prison in Berlin. In January 1945, Eugen was sent to a building where he was confined with Jews who had been found hiding in the Berlin area. He saw his mother there, and they stayed together until she was sent to

Opposite: Berlin, Germany, August 1945.

Theresienstadt. Eugen was kept in prisons in Berlin until the end of the war.

Eugen and his mother both survived. His father died. He may have taken his own life by swallowing poison he had secretly obtained.

The war was over before Ruth's father and other members of the Association could be put on trial. Ruth's father was freed from prison by American soldiers. After the war, he was reunited with his family. Horst died at the age of twenty-eight after an illness.

Today Ruth is married to Gerd Kühne. They live in Berlin.

chapter eight

Honor and Controversy

Some people who were saved by non-Jews are grateful but are ambivalent about honoring their rescuers publicly. They fear the public will forget that cruelty was much more common than kindness during the period of Nazi terror. To honor the Righteous Gentiles seems to some survivors to overlook the fact that most non-Jews did little or nothing to stop the horror.

The vast majority of non-Jews in Germany, Austria, and German-occupied lands did not protest when they saw persecution, even if it bothered them. For many, it was just easier not to do anything about it. That made it easier for the Nazis to carry out their deadly policies. Eventually, resistance to Nazi policies was punishable by death.

But still, a tiny few in all those countries did resist.

Their courageous efforts must be remembered. Their faces are everyday faces, and their words are matter-of-fact. But the acts of those who rescued Jews during World War II are far from common when illuminated by the Nazi searchlight.

German civilians from the area surrounding Buchenwald are forced by
American soldiers to see the corpses of prisoners killed in the camp.

chapter nine

Preserving the Memories

Many people who experienced the years of Nazi terror have had trouble talking about it in later years. For some, the memories are just too painful, and they fear letting these memories interfere with a normal life.

Recently, though, more and more survivors and witnesses are deciding that it is time to record their memories, so their experiences will never be forgotten or denied. Sometimes, they talk with their own children or with high school students. Tens of thousands of survivors have recorded their memories on videotape.

Preben Munch-Nielsen now runs a successful business in Denmark. "The lessons of the past are relevant today," he says. He knows most teens don't have to risk their lives every day the way teens under Nazi occupation did. But they have challenges of their own.

He encourages teens, saying it is "easy to make the right decision," especially when it comes to respecting differences between people. "The more you know about your fellow citizen, the less you fear," he says.

Niels Bamberger now lives in the United States, where he, too, runs a business. He reflects on the country that saved his life and the lives of thousands of his fellow citizens. "The Danes are a great people and one of the few nations that did more than their share to help the Jews all over the world. I am sure they would do it today again if it happened; they would be willing to help with money, deeds, and everything. They are very unselfish and they are not asking for any thank

American soldiers walk past rows of corpses that have been removed from the camp barracks to their left. Nordhausen, Germany, April 1945.

you or anything in public by anyone. They never did."

Teresa Prekerowa did not tell her parents the story of her having hidden the little girl until after the war. "They were very angry that I did not tell them at the time, and they said that of course they would have kept the girl despite the danger."

After the war, Teresa said, Warsaw was changed. "Everyday problems filled the life. And the environment changed. Warsaw was totally destroyed in 1944. It was rebuilt, but it is not the same town as in 1943."

Teresa became a professor of history. Her work was affected by the war. "As a historian I write about the Holocaust and the fate of

Preben Munch-Nielsen with President Clinton at Memorial Park, Denmark, July 10th, 1997.

Polish Jews," she said. "I think that the choice of this subject was influenced by the terrible events of the Second World War." Professor Prekerowa died in spring 1998.

Ruth Winkler-Kühne's father, Hans Winkler, died in 1987, and her mother, Frida, in 1988. Eugen Herman-Friede survived and lives in Germany today. In 1991, his book about his experience in hiding was published. It is called *No Time for Joy*. Ruth became a shopkeeper in a candy store. She married Gerd Kühne in 1993.

"There are many people today who say, 'We could have done more' to save people," Ruth says. "They have a bad conscience. When Germans say to me, 'We didn't know about the gas chambers,' I have to laugh at them. I knew about these things already as a child. Where were they taking the Jews? No one asked what had happened to their former friends. No one said, 'Give me the address of my friends.' Everyone only thought about their own comfortable life.

"My parents helped and there were others who helped. But there were also millions who did not."

Timeline

January 30, 1933	Adolf Hitler is appointed Chancellor of Germany.
March 23, 1933	Dachau, the first concentration camp, is built to hold political opponents of Nazis.
April 1, 1933	Nazis proclaim a daylong boycott of Jewish-owned businesses.
July 14, 1933	Nazis outlaw all other political parties in Germany; a law is passed legalizing forced sterilization of Roma and Sinti ("Gypsies"), mentally and physically disabled Germans, African-Germans, and others.
January 26, 1934	Germany and Poland sign Non-Aggression Pact.
August 1, 1935	"No Jews" signs appear in Germany forbidding Jews from stores, restaurants, places of entertainment, etc.
September 15, 1935	German parliament passes the Nuremberg Laws.
March 13, 1938	Germany annexes Austria.
September 29, 1938	Munich Conference: Britain and France allow Hitler to annex part of Czechoslovakia in order to prevent war.
November 9, 1938	Kristallnacht (looting and vandalism of Jewish homes and businesses and wholesale destruction of synagogues) occurs throughout Germany and Austria; 30,000 Jews are sent to Nazi concentration camps.
March 15, 1939	Germany invades all of Czechoslovakia.
August 23, 1939	Germany and Soviet Union sign Non-Aggression Pact.
September 1, 1939	Germany invades western Poland.
September 2, 1939	Great Britain and France declare war on Germany.

September 17, 1939	Soviet Union invades eastern Poland.
Spring 1940	Germany invades Denmark, Norway, Holland, Luxembourg, Belgium, and France.
March 24, 1941	Germany invades North Africa.
April 6, 1941	Germany invades Yugoslavia and Greece.
June 22, 1941	Germany invades western Soviet Union.
July 31, 1941	Reinhard Heydrich appointed to carry out the "Final Solution" (extermination of all European Jews).
Summer 1941	*Einsatzgruppen* (mobile killing squads) begin to massacre Jews in western Soviet Union.
December 7, 1941	Japan bombs Pearl Harbor; United States enters World War II.
January 20, 1942	Wannsee Conference: Nazi leaders meet to design "Final Solution."
Spring and Summer 1942	Many Polish ghettos emptied; residents deported to death camps.
February 2, 1943	German troops in Stalingrad, Soviet Union, surrender; the Allies begin to win the war.
June 11, 1943	Nazis decide that all ghettos in Poland and Soviet Union are to be emptied and residents deported to death camps.
September 1943	Non-Jewish Danes help Danish Jews escape to Sweden to avoid being deported to concentration camps by the Nazis.
March 19, 1944	Germany occupies Hungary.
June 6, 1944	D-Day in Europe: Invasion of Normandy, France, by the Allies.
January 27, 1945	Soviet troops liberate Auschwitz
May 8, 1945	Germany surrenders to the Allies; war ends in Europe.

Glossary

antisemitism Hostility toward or discrimination against Jews.

Aryans According to Nazi idcology, a person of Nordic or Germanic background, a member of Hitler's "master race."

Bund Deutsche Mädel (League of German Girls) A Nazi youth group for "Aryan" German girls.

collaborators Non-Germans who willingly helped or supported the Nazis.

concentration camps A camp in which people live in inhumane conditions and may be killed by starvation, exhaustion, disease, torture, or execution.

death camps Concentration camps where people considered unfit for work or racially undesirable are murdered.

deportation The forced removal of people from one area to another.

Einsatzgruppen Mobile killing squads who killed Jews in lands occupied by the Germans.

gas chambers A room where people are killed by poison gas.

Gestapo The Nazi secret state police.

ghetto A part of a city set aside by the Nazis to contain only Jews. Ghettos were heavily guarded and lacking in food, water, heat, housing, and health care.

Hitler Youth A Nazi youth group that taught Nazi ideology and prepared German boys to become soldiers.

Holocaust The extermination of six million Jews and millions of others during World War II.

Kristallnacht Meaning the "night of broken glass," November 9, 1938, was a government-sponsored attack on Jews, resulting in the destruction of Jewish-owned businesses and synagogues.

Mischling A person with mixed Jewish and non-Jewish blood.

Nazis The political party that ruled in Germany (1933–1945); full name: National Socialist German Workers' Party.

Nuremberg Laws German laws passed on September 15, 1935, that legalized antisemitism and stripped Jewish Germans of many rights.

occupation The control of an area by a foreign military force.

Orthodox The most observant form of Judaism.

Reich The German word for "empire." Hitler called the period of Nazi control of Germany the Third Reich, which he claimed would last for 1,000 years.

Resistance Organized opposition, often in secret, to the ruling political party or leader.

show trial A trial, often of opponents of the government in power, in which the verdict has been decided before the trial begins.

synagogue A Jewish place of worship.

Torah Jewish holy writings that set out the laws and practices of Judaism.

transit camp (*Durchgangslager*) A camp where prisoners were held before being sent to a labor camp.

underground A network of organizations, usually secret, that act in opposition to the ruling political party or leader.

World War I The war in Europe that lasted from 1914 to 1918.

World War II The most devastating war in human history, which lasted from 1939 to 1945 and involved countries all over the world.

For Further Reading

Adler, David. *We Remember the Holocaust.* New York: Henry Holt and Company, 1989.

Altschuler, David A. *Hitler's War Against the Jews.* West Orange, NJ: Behrman House, 1978.

Bachrach, Susan D. *Tell Them We Remember: The Story of the Holocaust.* New York: Little, Brown & Co., 1994.

Drucker, Malka, and Michael Halperin. *Jacob's Rescue: A Holocaust Story.* New York: Bantam Doubleday Dell, 1993.

Eliach, Yaffa. *Hasidic Tales of the Holocaust.* New York: Random House, 1988.

Fogelman, Eva. *Conscience and Courage: Rescuers of Jews During the Holocaust.* New York: Doubleday, 1995.

Frank, Anne. *Diary of a Young Girl: The Definitive Edition.* New York: Doubleday, 1995.

Holliday, Laurel. *Children in the Holocaust and World War II: Their Secret Diaries.* New York: Washington Square Press, 1994.

Klein, Gerda. *All but My Life.* New York: Hill & Wang, 1995.

Lowry, Lois. *Number the Stars.* Boston: Houghton Mifflin, 1989.

Marks, Jane. *The Hidden Children: The Secret Survivors of the Holocaust.* New York: Ballantine Books, 1993.

Matas, Carol. *Lisa's War.* New York: Scribner, 1987.

Rochman, Hazel, and Darlene Z. McCampbell, eds. *Bearing Witness: Stories of the Holocaust.* New York: Orchard Books Watts, 1995.

Volavková, Hana. *I Never Saw Another Butterfly: Children's Drawings and Poems from Theresienstadt Concentration Camp.* New York: Schocken Books, 1994.

For Advanced Readers

Baumel, Judith Tydor. *Unfulfilled Promise: Rescue and Resettlement of Jewish Refugee Children in the United States, 1934–1945.* Juneau, Alaska: Denali Press 1990.

Edelheit, Abraham J., and Herschel Edelheit. *History of the Holocaust: A Handbook and Dictionary.* Boulder, CO: Westview Press, 1994.

Gilbert, Martin. *The Holocaust: A History of the Jews of Europe During the Second World War.* New York: Henry Holt & Co., 1985.

Meltzer, Milton. *Rescue: The Story of How Gentiles Saved Jews in the Holocaust.* New York: Harper & Row, 1988.

Rittner, Carol, and Sondra Myers, eds. *The Courage to Care: Rescuers of Jews During the Holocaust.* New York: New York University Press, 1986.

Roberts, Jack L. *Oscar Schindler.* San Diego, CA: Lucent Books, 1996.

Videos

The Courage to Care
This documentary features interviews with and information about ordinary people who stood up to Nazi tyranny and helped victims of the Holocaust, at great risk to their own lives. Nominated for an Academy Award. (Available from Zenger Videos, 10200 Jefferson Boulevard, Room J, P. O. Box 802, Culver City, CA 90232; (800) 421-4246.)

The Other Side of Faith
Seen from a first-person perspective, this film tells the true story of a remarkable Polish Catholic teenager who hid thirteen Jews in her attic. Filmed on location in Przemysl, Poland. (Available from Film and Video Foundation, 1800 K Street, Suite 1120, Washington, DC 20006; (202) 429-9320.)

Weapons of the Spirit
This documentary tells the moving story of the French village of Le Chambon-sur-Lignon. The mostly Protestant townspeople there, under the leadership of Pastor André Trocmé, gave refuge to about 5,000 Jews during World War II. (Available from Zenger Video, 10200 Jefferson Boulevard, Room J, P. O. Box 802, Culver City, CA 90232; (800) 421-4246.)

Shoah
This film includes interviews with victims, perpetrators, and bystanders, and takes viewers to camps, towns, and railways that were part of the Holocaust. (Available in most video stores and many libraries.)

Web Sites

Anti-Defamation League—Braun Holocaust Institute
http://www.adl.org/Braun/braun.htm

Cybrary of the Holocaust
http://www.remember.org

Holocaust Education and Memorial Centre of Toronto
http://www.feduja.org

Museum of Tolerance
www.wiesenthal.com/mot/index.html

Simon Wiesenthal Center
http://www.wiesenthal.com/

United States Holocaust Memorial Museum
http://www.ushmm.org/index.html

Yad Vashem
http://www.yad-vashem.org.il

Index

A

Association for Peace and
    Reconstruction, 44, 48, 49

B

Bamberger, Niels, 35–42, 53–54
Best, Dr. Werner, 28–29

C

Copenhagen, 35, 36

D

Danish Brigade, 32
Denmark, 26–33, 38, 39, 40, 41,
    53, 54
    German occupation of,
        26, 27–29, 38
deportation, 18, 26, 29
Duckwitz, G. F., 29

G

Germany, 11, 12, 13, 14, 18, 28
    antisemitism in, 13, 14, 15,
        17
    Jews in, 13, 15, 17

H

Herman-Friede, Eugen, 43, 44,
    45, 46, 49
Hitler, Adolf, 11, 12, 28–29, 46;
    ideology, 12–13, 14, 15, 18

K

Kristallnacht, 17, 46

L

Luckenwalde, Germany, 43, 46,
    48

M

Munch-Nielsen, Preben, 26–33,
    52, 53

N

Nazis, 6, 7, 9, 10, 11, 12, 17, 18, 22
Nuremberg Laws, 17

P

Poland, 9, 14, 18, 21, 22
Prekerowa, Teresa, 22–25, 54
punishment for hiding Jews, 9,
    10, 11, 17, 22, 24

R

resistance, 20, 43, 48;
 in Denmark, 28, 29, 30, 31
Righteous Among the Nations
  (Righteous Gentiles), 7, 9,
  11, 17, 20, 21, 51
Roma and Sinti ("Gypsies"), 18
Roslan, Alexander, 9
Roslan, Jerzy, 9

S

Snekkersten, Denmark, 26, 29,
  32, 39
Sweden, 26, 29, 30, 32, 40, 41

T

Theresienstadt, 33, 44, 49
Third Reich, 11, 21

W

Warsaw ghetto, 22
Winkler, Hans, 43, 44, 48, 49, 54
Winkler-Kühne, Ruth, 43–50, 54

Y

Yad Vashem, 9, 11, 20

About the Author

Toby Axelrod is a 1997-98 Fulbright scholar and was an award-winning journalist for the New York *Jewish Week*. Born in Queens, New York, she studied at Vassar College and the Columbia University Graduate School of Journalism. She is currently writing a book about how young Germans today are confronting their own family involvement in Nazi crimes.

About the Series Editor

Yaffa Eliach is Professor of History and Literature in the Department of Judaic Studies at Brooklyn College. She founded and directed the Center for Holocaust Studies (now part of the Museum of Jewish Heritage—A Living Memorial to the Holocaust) and created the Tower of Life exhibit at the U.S. Holocaust Memorial Museum. Professor Eliach's book *There Once Was a World: A Nine Hundred Year Chronicle of the Shtetl of Eishyshok* was a finalist for the 1998 National Book Award for Nonfiction. She is also the author of *Hasidic Tales of the Holocaust; We Were Children Just Like You;* and *The Liberators: Eyewitness Accounts of the Liberation of Concentration Camps.*

Photo Credits
P. 6-7 © Ghetto Fighters' Museum, courtesy of the United States Holocaust Memorial Museum (USHMM) Photo Archives; p. 8 © Maria Austria Institute, courtesy of USHMM Photo Archives; p. 10 © Dokumentationsarchiv des Osterreichischen, courtesy of USHMM Photo Archives; p. 12 © Leo Baeck Institute, courtesy of USHMM Photo Archives; p. 13 © courtesy of USHMM Photo Archives; pp. 14, 15 National Archives, courtesy of USHMM Photo Archives; pp. 16, 23 © Yad Vashem Jerusalem, courtesy of USHMM Photo Archives; pp. 18-19, 36-37 © Main Commission for the Investigation of Nazi War Crimes, courtesy of USHMM Photo Archives; pp. 20, 40 © OFRIHEDSMUSEET, courtesy of USHMM Photo Archives; pp. 22, 44-45, 47 © Archive Photos; pp. 24-25 courtesy of Sisters of Nazareth Convent, Warsaw, Poland; pp. 27, 28 © The National Archives/CORBIS-Bettman; pp. 30-31 © Grant Smith courtesy of CORBIS-Bettman; pp. 32, 34-35 © UPI/CORBIS-Bettman; p. 39 © Yivo Institute for Jewish Research, courtesy of USHMM Photo Archives; pp. 41, 42 courtesey of Ruth Winkler-Kühne; p. 49 © Anne Morrison, courtesy of USHMM Photo Archives; pp. 50-51 © Donald S. Robinson Collection, courtesy of USHMM Photo Archives; p. 52 courtesy of Preben Munch-Nielsen.

Series Design
Kim Sonsky

Layout
Oliver Halsman Rosenberg